I0878417

FAR-OUT and UNUSUAL pets

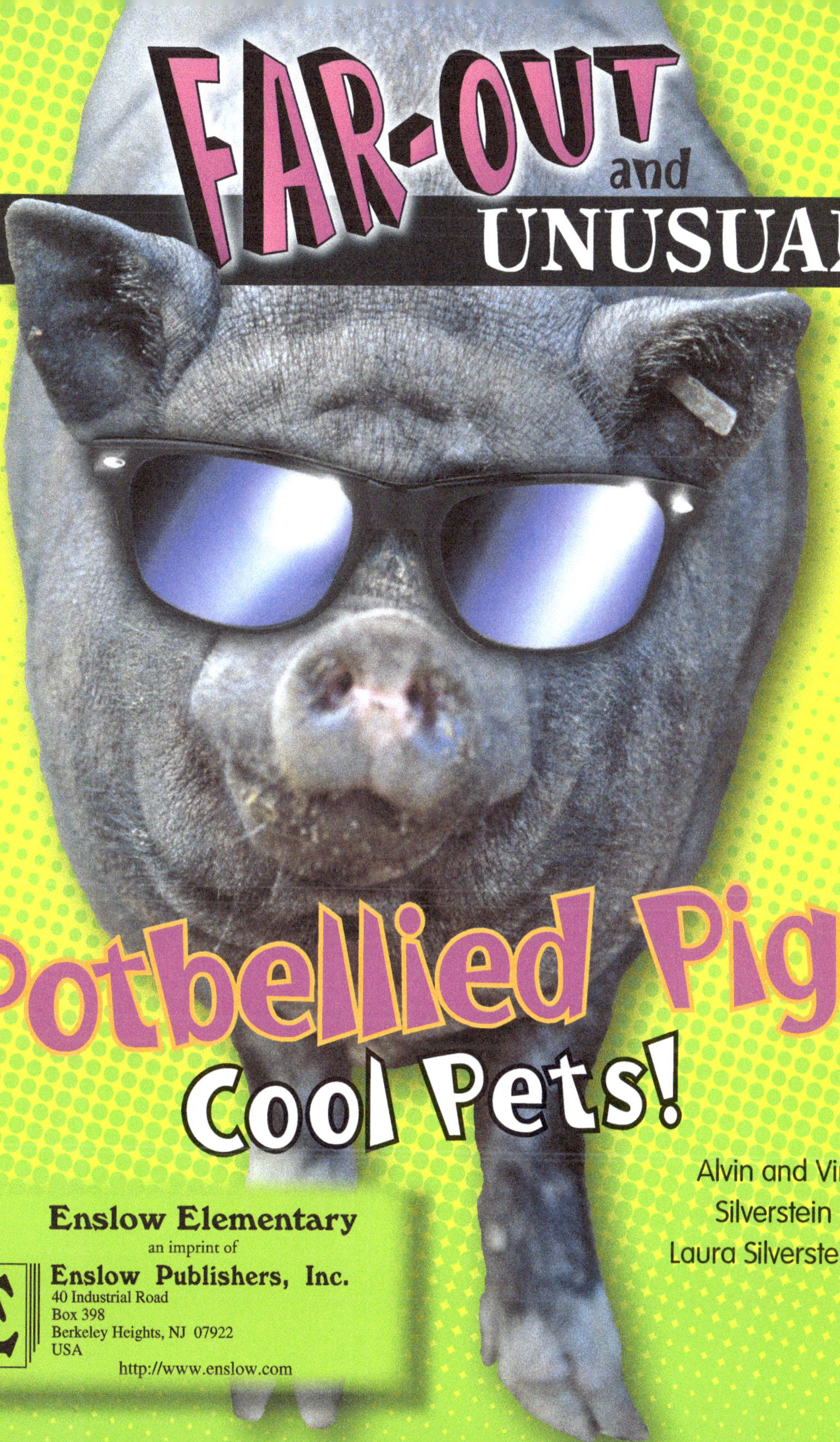

Potbellied Pigs

Cool Pets!

Alvin and Virginia Silverstein and Laura Silverstein Nunn

Enslow Elementary
an imprint of
Enslow Publishers, Inc.
40 Industrial Road
Box 398
Berkeley Heights, NJ 07922
USA
http://www.enslow.com

Copyright © 2011 by Alvin Silverstein, Virginia Silverstein, and Laura Silverstein Nunn

All rights reserved.

No part of this book may be reproduced by any means
without the written permission of the publisher.

Library of Congress Cataloging-in-Publication Data

Silverstein, Alvin.
Potbellied pigs : cool pets! / by Alvin Silverstein, Virginia Silverstein, and Laura Silverstein Nunn.
p. cm. — (Far-out and unusual pets)
Includes bibliographical references and index.
Summary: "Provides basic information about potbellied pigs and keeping them as pets"—Provided by publisher.
ISBN 978-0-7660-3687-1
1. Potbellied pigs as pets—Juvenile literature. I. Silverstein, Virginia B. II. Nunn, Laura Silverstein. III. Title.
SF393.P74S55 2012
636.4'85—dc22

2010001118

Printed in the United States of America

102010 Lake Book Manufacturing, Inc., Melrose Park, IL

10 9 8 7 6 5 4 3 2 1

To Our Readers: We have done our best to make sure all Internet Addresses in this book were active and appropriate when we went to press. However, the author and the publisher have no control over and assume no liability for the material available on those Internet sites or on other Web sites they may link to. Any comments or suggestions can be sent by e-mail to comments@enslow.com or to the address on the back cover.

Enslow Publishers, Inc., is committed to printing our books on recycled paper. The paper in every book contains 10% to 30% post-consumer waste (PCW). The cover board on the outside of each book contains 100% PCW. Our goal is to do our part to help young people and the environment too!

Photo credits: Alamy: © Andreas von Einsiedel, p. 29, © imagebroker, p. 17; Anthony Souffle/Post-Dispatch, p. 26; Ardea: © Duncan Usher p. 1, © Jean Michel Labat, p. 9; Associated Press, pp. 12, 44; Geoffrey Robinson/Rex USA/Courtesy Everett Collection, p. 18; © Image 100 Ltd., p. 24; iStockphoto: © Duncan Astbury, pp. 1, 19, © Jason Rowland, p. 35, © Jennifer Daley, p. 20; © Mark Richards/PhotoEdit, p. 43; © PhotoDisc, p. 45; Photolibrary: age footstock, p. 22, Mauritius, p. 4; Shutterstock.com, pp. 1 (sunglasses), 3, 6 (both), 15; STAN HONDA/AFP/Getty Images, p. 37; Westend61/Punchstock, p. 32.

Cover Photo: © Duncan Usher/Ardea; Shutterstock.com (sunglasses).

Illustration Credits: © 2010 Gerald Kelley, www.geraldkelley.com

Contents

A potbellied piglet makes
a good and loyal pet.

1

Miniature Pigs

A pig for a pet? Don't pigs live on a farm? Actually, farm pigs would not make very good pets. They are huge—up to 1,500 pounds (680 kg)! Imagine trying to cuddle up to that at night. It would break your bed!

The kind of pig we're talking about is a potbellied pig. Potbellied pigs are much smaller than farm pigs. These miniature pigs make much better pets. They usually weigh no more than 150 pounds (68 kg). That's less than what some dogs weigh! Pet owners say that potbellied pigs are super smart and just as loyal as dogs.

Far Out!

How Much Does It Weigh?

A potbellied pig weighs less than a Saint Bernard. The Saint Bernard is one of the largest dog breeds. Male pigs can weigh up to 200 pounds (91 kg) or more!

A potbellied pig is a really cool pet. It will follow you around like a dog. It can even learn to do tricks. But potbellied pigs are not right for everyone. They are a huge responsibility. They need plenty of love, attention, and training.

Read on to find out what makes a potbellied pig such a far-out and unusual pet.

2

The First Pig Pets

Keeping pigs as pets is not a new idea. Some books say that pigs were first tamed in China 8,000 years ago. These were probably potbellied pigs. The ancient Chinese raised pigs as food animals, but they kept some as pets. The first book on raising pigs was written more than 5,000 years ago. Around 1,000 years ago, potbellied pigs had already been tamed in many countries of Asia.

In the 1950s, Vietnamese potbellied pigs were brought to Europe. They reached North America in the 1980s. It didn't take long before the pigs became hugely popular.

Far Out!

Pigs in the Family

In ancient Asia, people treated potbellied pigs like members of the family. At mealtimes they gave their pigs table scraps to eat. They even bathed them in bath water that had been used for the children.

Coming to America

In the 1950s, a number of potbellied pigs were sent to Sweden. They were part of a zoo collection of animals from Asia. In 1985, Keith Connell brought eighteen potbellied pigs from Europe into Canada. Connell was a Canadian zoo director. He bred the pigs, and soon new potbellies were born. These pigs were mostly black and wrinkled, especially on the head and face. Connell sent some of his pigs to zoos in the United States.

Within a few years, pet breeders in the United States were raising potbellied pigs, too. The black, wrinkly pigs that came from Connell's group became known as the Con Line.

Since the 1980s, potbellied pigs have been popular pets in the United States.

Other breeders also brought potbellied pigs from Europe to the United States. Keith Leavitt, in Texas, started the Lea Line in 1989. These pigs had white and black markings. They were very gentle and somewhat smaller than Connell's pigs.

Another breeder raised pigs that were mostly white, but a little larger than Leavitt's pigs. This group became known as the Royal Line.

Most of the potbellied pigs in the United States today come from the Con Line, the Lea Line, or the Royal Line.

The Pig Craze

By the early 1990s, the potbellied pig was the new "must have" pet. People saw the baby pigs and just fell in love with them. These piglets were so small you could hold them in your hands. Who could resist?

At the time, there was not much information about keeping potbellied pigs as pets. How do you take care of them? Where do they sleep? How do

Pricey Pigs

At first, potbellied pigs were pets only the rich could afford. A pregnant potbellied pig could be sold for more than $20,000! Eventually, the prices dropped. Now, they usually cost less than $1,000.

you train them? When people brought their new pet pigs home, they had to figure out a lot of that on their own.

Many pet owners didn't know how to deal with their pigs. They couldn't get the pig to do what they wanted it to do. The animal was out of

Owners who did not learn how to care for their potbellied pigs abandoned them at shelters.

control. It was tearing up the owner's home, ripping up clothes, and destroying furniture.

Many owners just gave up. They dropped off their pigs at animal shelters. In fact, there were so many that animal rescue organizations set up special shelters just for potbellied pigs.

It wasn't really the pigs' fault. Potbellies *could* be good pets . . . if only their owners knew how to care for them. Soon pig experts were writing books and pamphlets on how to raise and train potbellied pigs. The Internet has also made it very easy to find information.

3

Are You Ready for a Potbellied Pig?

When a potbellied pig is born, it is small enough to hold in the palm of your hand. This tiny pig would make an adorable little pet. But potbellied piglets don't stay tiny for long. They grow quickly. A year-old potbellied pig weighs more than one hundred times its weight at birth!

By the time you get your potbellied pig, at about eight to ten weeks old, it will no longer be a cute

Newborn piglets are very cute. But beware, that newborn pig could reach 150 pounds (680 kg) in just three years!

Far Out!

See How the Little Piggy Grows*

	Height at Shoulder	Weight
At Birth	2-3 inches (5-8 cm)	6-8 ounces (170-227 grams)
1 Year	12 inches (30 cm)	60-70 pounds (27-32 kg)
2 Years	14 inches (36 cm)	80-90 pounds (36-41 kg)
3 Years	16 inches (41 cm)	100-125 pounds (45-57 kg)

*Averages for pet potbellied pigs in the United States, according to the National Potbellied Pig Registry.

little pocket pet. You can still scoop it up and cuddle it. But when it is a year old, it may be too heavy for you to lift. And you will soon find out that your adorable pig pet can make a big mess—in your house and out in the backyard.

Are you really ready for a potbellied pig? The best thing you can do for yourself and your pig is learn everything you can. Where should you get your pig? How do you take care of it? How do you train it? Be prepared.

The Potbellied Pig Up Close

A potbellied pig is short and chubby. It is about 12 to 16 inches (30 to 41 cm) tall at the shoulders. Its round "potbelly" gives it its name. When the pig is full grown, it will probably weigh between 100 and 150 pounds (45 to 68 kg). Potbellied pigs over 200 pounds (91 kg) are usually overweight.

Potbellied pigs get their name from their big, round "potbellies."

Some breeders raise miniature "teacup" pigs.

Far Out!

Teacup Pigs

Some breeders sell "teacup" or "micro mini" pigs. They call them teacup pigs because the piglets are small enough to fit in a teacup. These breeders believe that pig pets would be even more popular if they were a super small breed. But potbellied pigs that weigh less than 40 pounds (18 kg) as adults are usually not healthy. Often these tiny pigs are actually underfed.

The first pet potbellied pigs in North America were jet black. But breeding with white and spotted pigs has led to other color patterns, many of which include black, white, tan, and silver (gray). A pig doesn't have soft hair or fur like a cat or dog. It has short, stiff hairs, called bristles. It grows a longer coat of bristles in the fall and winter. In the summer, the pig sheds its coat.

Potbellied pigs may be black, white, tan, silver, or even spotted.

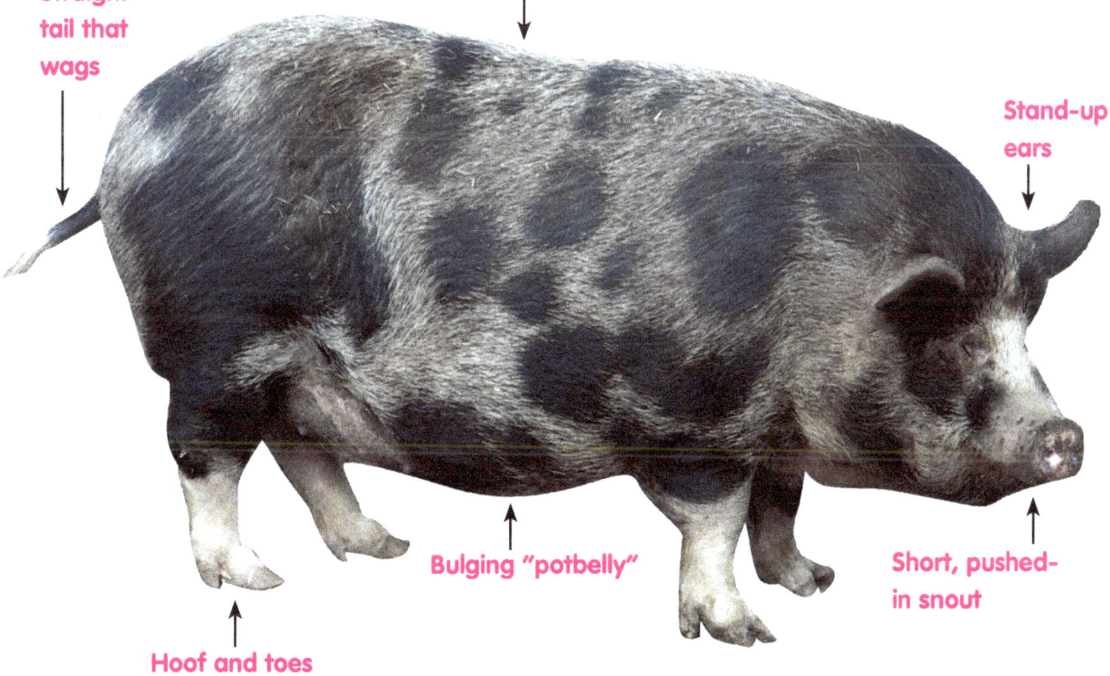

Short, pushed-in snouts and bristly hairs are features of potbellied pigs.

A potbellied pig is not really a miniature *copy* of a farm pig. Its short, wrinkled, pushed-in nose is smaller than most farm pig snouts. The potbellied pig's small ears stand up straight. Instead of a curly tail, it has a straight tail that wags like a dog's tail.

A potbellied pig can bark like a dog, too. It barks to warn of danger, and it squeals when it is excited or hurt. This little pig also "talks" by making little grunts and honking sounds.

Like all pigs, potbellies grow tusks. These are long, pointed teeth that are used for digging. Females have small tusks. But males' tusks are much larger. By about three years of age, the tusks are long enough to stick out of the male pig's mouth.

A potbellied pig has four toes on each foot. It uses the two large middle ones for walking. It actually walks on hooves, a hard covering over each of the toes.

A potbellied pig uses its tusks for digging.

Far Out!

Pigs of the Stars

Rupert Grint, the actor who plays Ron Weasley in the Harry Potter movies, owns a potbellied pig. In Britain, where he lives, potbellied pigs are hugely popular as pets. American actor George Clooney had a potbellied pig named Max. Max lived for about eighteen years. He weighed nearly three hundred pounds when he died.

Where to Buy a Potbellied Pig

Before you run out and buy a pig, you must first find out if potbellied pigs are allowed as pets where you live. Many cities and towns have laws against keeping livestock—farm animals like cattle, sheep, and chickens. Since pigs are farm animals, these laws may mean that even miniature pigs cannot be kept as pets. However, the potbellied pig's popularity has helped change the laws in many places.

Once you find out that you can keep potbellied pigs in your town, where do you get one?

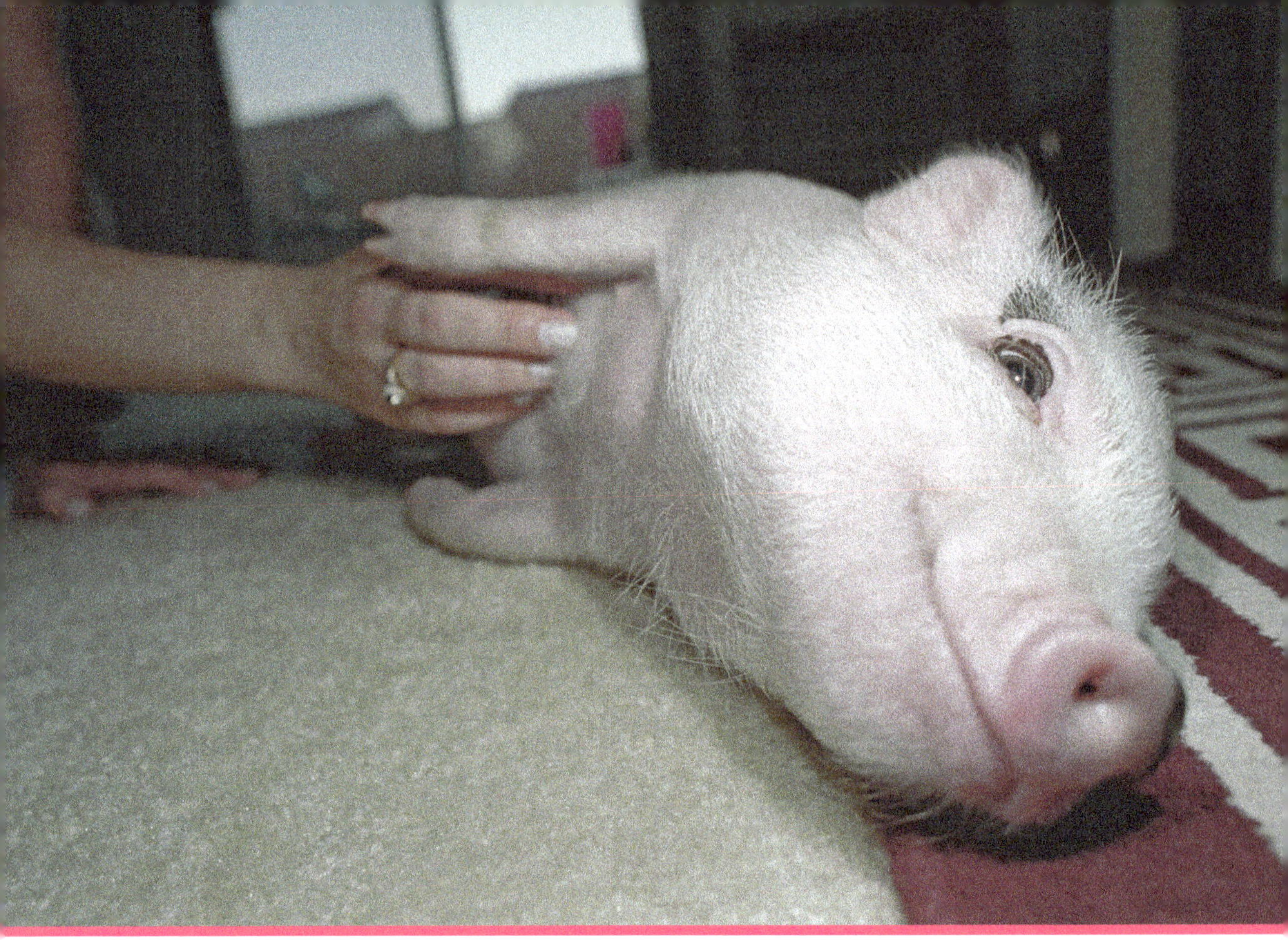

Before you bring a potbellied pig into your home, make sure they are allowed as pets in your town.

You can't pick one up at the local pet store. Most pet shops do not sell miniature pigs. Many states have laws against selling farm animals in stores. But you can find potbelly breeders and rescue shelters on the Internet.

4

Caring for a Potbellied Pig

Can a potbellied pig fit into your family as easily as a pet dog or cat? Like dogs, pigs are social animals. In the wild, they live in groups. Wild pigs love to snuggle up together. Potbellies are just as friendly. When raised as pets, they are loving with people. They can learn to get along happily with your family.

There's a lot to think about before you get a potbellied pig. Where will you keep it? Will it stay inside the house or in an outside shed? Have you

A potbellied pig can make a fun and unusual addition to your family.

stocked up on potbellied pig feed? How will you keep the pig from getting bored while you're gone during the day? Don't wait until after you bring home your new pet to make such important decisions.

Indoors or Outdoors?

Baby pigs should be kept indoors. Growing up in your family's home can help them feel loved and secure. It will also help your pet develop a strong bond with you. As the pig grows to full-size, though, it may be time to let it spend more time outside. Eventually, you might want to keep it in an outdoor shelter.

Keeping your pig indoors? You'll need to "pig proof" your home. Don't let the pig have the run of the entire house. Keep it in a safe room where there are no breakable objects or electrical cords.

Your pig's bed should be made up of blankets and pillows. It is best to get inexpensive blankets.

Can Potbellied Pigs Get Along With Other Pets?

Not always. If a cat gets annoyed, it will probably just walk away. But dogs are different. Pigs and dogs can get along, but they should never be left alone together. Even a sweet-natured dog may suddenly attack a pig—especially if food is involved!

The pig will probably rip them apart to make its own bed the way it wants it.

If you leave your potbellied pet alone all day, it will get bored. Pigs are very smart and curious. They can easily find things to do to pass the time. Unfortunately, this can lead to a huge mess.

Give your pig inexpensive pillows and blankets so that it can make itself a comfy bed.

Potbellied pigs have been known to rip up rugs or carpets, scratch up floors, and chew on walls. They can even open kitchen cupboards and pull things out onto the floor. Many have figured out how to open up a refrigerator!

You can help keep your pig from getting bored by giving it cheap toys to play with. Potbellied pigs like to play with balls, buckets, and cardboard boxes. Paper bags stuffed with newspapers, with a few food pellets mixed in, also make good toys. Your pig would be happy with dog toys, too.

Far Out!

Safety First!

Potbellied pigs are like young children. They can get into everything. You need to make your home safe, the way parents would do for their child. Remove cleaning supplies, insect sprays, and other harmful substances from lower cabinets. It might help to put safety latches on the cabinets so the pig can't get into them.

You may want to keep your potbellied pig in a comfortable place outdoors.

Pigs are easy to housebreak. They can learn to use a litter box. Or they will learn to pace back and forth by the door when they need to go outside.

Indoor pigs should never be kept inside *all* the time. It is the pig's nature to want to be outside. If it stays indoors too long, it may become restless. Take your potbellied pig on walks. Let it run around in a fenced-in backyard. But be aware that your nice-looking lawn and garden won't stay that way with a pig around. Pigs love to "root," or dig in the ground with their snouts. Soon the lawn or garden will be full of holes!

What if you decide to keep your potbellied pig outdoors? Outdoor pigs need a fenced-in area where they can play. There should be some shady spots for the pig to rest or just hang out. For night time and bad weather, potbellied pigs need a weatherproof shed or barn. Lots of blankets and straw can help keep them warm at night.

When the weather is warm, pigs like to cool down in a nice pool of . . . mud! Yes, mud. If they

Rooting Around

Pigs like to dig holes because some tasty stuff grows underground. Many of these foods, such as sweet potatoes and turnips, are plant roots. In Europe, farmers use pigs to dig up truffles, a very expensive kind of mushroom that people eat. Pigs have such a keen sense of smell that they can sniff out food growing underground.

can find it, they will roll in it. Soon they will be covered in wet, sticky mud. They may look awfully dirty, but the mud makes them feel cool and comfortable. A coat of caked-on mud also protects them from biting insects. It helps protect their skin from the sun, too. That's good, since pigs can get sunburned!

Pigs don't have to roll in mud to stay cool. If you want to keep your pig clean, keep a child's plastic wading pool with water in the backyard.

Eating Like a Pig

"You are such a pig!" That's what people say when someone eats a lot. So are pigs really that "piggish" when it comes to food? Actually, yes.

If there's one thing pigs love, it's food! They will root around your backyard looking for food. They will turn over your couch cushions or dump out your wastebasket just to find something to eat. Pigs will eat and eat and eat—if you let them. So when it's feeding time, don't overdo it! If the pig becomes overweight, it could develop health problems. But don't underfeed it, either. Pigs need enough food for their bodies to grow normally.

What do potbellied pigs eat? In the wild, pigs eat plants, fruits, insects, roots, or anything else

Leafy greens and crunchy vegetables are good treats for potbellied pigs.

they can find in the forest. But pet pigs usually eat pig chow. This is a food made especially for potbellied pigs. You can find it at feed stores. Do not give your pig cat or dog food or table scraps, though. These will add extra pounds to your pig.

Potbellied pigs should have some fruits and vegetables in their diet. Give them leafy vegetables, such as lettuce and spinach. They enjoy crunching on apples, too. They may also want to graze on grass.

Your pet will need some water to drink when it's thirsty. Keep it in a bowl that won't tip over.

5

Training Your Pig

Everybody knows that dogs can be taught to obey commands, such as "sit," "stay," and "come." Yet pigs are just as smart as dogs and can learn to obey these commands, too! In fact, you would be surprised at all the things a potbellied pig can learn to do. But training a pig isn't all about teaching it to do tricks. Actually, training is *very* important in teaching your pig to be a good pet.

Who's the Boss?

You have to be firm with a pet potbelly from the beginning. In the wild, a pig lives in a herd—a group of pigs. The pig sees your family as its herd.

But in a real herd, some pigs may become mean and nasty toward other pigs. They may bite and push others around. It is their way of trying to show who's "top pig." Your pig may try to test your family to see who's boss.

The first word your pig has to learn is "No." It needs to know that you are in charge. Don't allow your pet to do whatever it wants, whenever it wants. Otherwise, it will quickly turn into a spoiled pig. It will demand constant attention and try to boss the family around. This can get scary when it grows up. The pig may bite or even charge at you. Eventually, it will end up destroying your house.

Trick *and* Treat

The best way to train potbellied pigs—or any pets for that matter—is to give them treats. Food makes the perfect treat. You may use fruit or dry cereal, or something else your pig likes. When the pig does what you want it to, reward it with a treat.

Don't Get Tricked!

Potbellied pigs will do just about anything for a treat. But don't use treats to housebreak your pig. Soon the pig will pretend to go potty just to get a treat!

Use a lot of praise, too, when the pig does something right.

Pigs can learn to come when they are called, sit up and beg, roll over, dance, climb stairs, and catch a frisbee. With a harness and leash you can take a pet potbelly for a walk. Some pigs have even

Reward your pig for obeying commands and you could teach it to perform all kinds of tricks.

Potbellied pigs are so smart, they can even learn to jump through hoops!

learned to ride a skateboard! Some can jump through hoops.

Training potbellied pigs takes a lot of work and patience. But in the end, it is well worth it. Your pig pet will snuggle up and watch TV with you or keep you company while you read. When you want to play, it will enjoy doing tricks for you—especially when food is involved! This is a pet that will stay around for a long time, too, with a lifespan of about fifteen years or more.

Words to Know

breed—To mate animals and raise their young; *also*, a group of animals with similar characteristics.

breeder—A person who breeds animals.

bristles—Short, stiff hairs.

herd—A group of the same kind of animals.

hoof (*plural* hooves)—The hard covering of the foot of animals such as horses, deer, and pigs.

miniature—A smaller form of something that is normally much larger.

rooting—Digging up the surface of the ground out of curiosity or in search of food.

tusk—A long, pointed tooth used for fighting or digging.

Learn More

Books

Binns, Tristan Boyer. *Potbellied Pigs.* Chicago: Heinemann Library, 2004.

Lunis, Natalie. *Potbellied Pigs.* New York: Bearport Publishing Company, Inc., 2010.

Valentine, Priscilla. *Potbellied Pig: Behavior and Training.* Spokane, Wash.: Luminary Media Group, 2005.

Web Sites

Pig Pals Sanctuary.
<http://www.pigpalssanctuary.com/index.htm>

Southern California Association for Miniature Potbellied Pigs.
<http://www.scampp.com/>

Index